OFFICIAL

Cambridge English

FUN
for Starters

Student's Book
Third edition

Anne Robinson
Karen Saxby

Cambridge University Press
www.cambridge.org/elt

Cambridge English Language Assessment
www.cambridgeenglish.org

Information on this title: www.cambridge.org/9781107444706

© Cambridge University Press 2015

First published 2006
Second edition 2010
Third edition 2015
5th printing 2015

Printed in Italy by Rotolito Lombarda S.p.A.

A catalogue record for this publication is available from the British Library

ISBN 978-1107-44470-6 Student's Book with audio and online activities
ISBN 978-1107-44472-0 Teacher's Book with audio
ISBN 978-1107-44476-8 Class Audio CD
ISBN 978-1107-48261-6 Presentation Plus DVD-ROM

Download the audio at www.cambridge.org/funfor

The authors and publishers would like to thank the ELT professionals who commented on the material at different stages of its development.

The authors are grateful to: Niki Donnelly of Cambridge University Press.

Anne Robinson would like to give special thanks to Adam Evans and her parents Margaret and Jim and to many, many teachers and students who have inspired her along the way. Special thanks to Cristina and Victoria for their help, patience and enthusiasm. And in memory of her brother Dave.

Karen Saxby would like to give special thanks to everyone she has worked with at Cambridge Assessment since the birth of YLE! She would particularly like to mention Frances, Felicity and Ann Kelly. She would also like to acknowledge the enthusiasm of all the teachers she has met through her work in this field. And lastly, Karen would like to say a big thank you to her sons, Tom and William, for bringing constant FUN and creative thinking to her life and work.

Editorial work by Bridget Kelly

Cover design by Crush Creative

Sound recordings by dsound Recording Studios, London

Book design and page make-up by emc design Ltd

The authors and publishers are grateful to the following illustrators:

T = Top, B = Below, L = Left, R = Right, C = Centre, B/G = Background

Laetitia Aynié (Sylvie Poggio Artists Agency) pp. 23 (C), 44 (T), 58 (C), 81 (T), 87 (T); David Banks pp. 58, 86 (B), 99 (B); Joanna Boccardo pp. 33 (C), 84 (T); Chris Embleton-Hall (Advocate Art) pp. 11 (T), 17 (C), 41 (B), 48, 67 (T), 76 (B), 94 (B); Andrew Elkerton (Sylvie Poggio Artists Agency) pp. 7, 9 (B), 13 (T), 16 (B), 17 (T, B), 33 (T), 34, 35, 54, 71 (T), 72 (T), 74 (C), 75 (B), 82 (C), 89, 94 (T); Clive Goodyer pp. 18, 19 (T), 25 (T), 26 (B), 27, 32 (B), 38 (B), 43 (B), 45, 69, 72 (B), 76 (T), 80 (T), 86 (T); Andrew Hamilton pp. 13 (B), 15 (T, B), 20 (T), 26, 32 (T), 41 (T), 44 (C), 46 (B), 47 (T), 61 (C, B), 68 (B), 78 (T), 84 (C), 88 (C); Brett Hudson (Graham-Cameron Illustration) pp. 19 (B), 37 (T), 49 (C), 50 (B), 53 (T), 79 (T); Kelly Kennedy (Sylvie Poggio Artists Agency) pp. 9 (T), 39 (T), 46 (T), 47 (B), 51 (T), 66, 68 (T), 73, 82 (B), 85; Nigel Kitching pp. 18 (T), 25 (C), 43 (T), 49 (B), 53 (BL), 57 (T), 61, 97 (T); Arpad Olbey (Beehive Illustration) pp. 19 (C), 10, 71 (C), 87 (B); Nina de Polonia (Advocate Art) pp. 10, 44 (B), 50 (T), 59, 62, 80 (B), 82 (T), 88 (B), 93 (B); David Pratt pp. 37 (B); Anthony Rule monkey and Project bag images throughout, pp. 5, 6, 11, 14, 18, 19, 22, 26, 31, 32, 38, 41, 46, 50, 55, 58, 62, 66, 68, 72, 74, 76, 78, 82, 86, 87, 90, 94; Pip Sampson pp. 15 (C), 29, 30, 38 (T), 40, 43 (C), 56, 57 (B), 63, 70, 71 (B), 74, 78 (B), 79 (B), 90; Melanie Sharp (Sylvie Poggio Artists Agency) pp. 6 (B), 8, 11 (R), 16 (T), 22, 23 (B), 37 (C), 52, 53 (BR), 60, 64, 65, 73, 77, 83, 88, 95, 97 (C, B), 99 (T); Emily Skinner pp. 57 (B); Jo Taylor pp. 20 (B), 21, 28, 31, 39 (B), 42, 58 (B), 74 (B), 75 (T), 81 (B), 84 (B), 91, 92; Theresa Tibbetts pp. 93 (T, C); Sue Wimperis (Graham-Cameron Illustration) pp. 67 (B); Sue Woollatt (Graham-Cameron Illustration) pp. 14, 34, 96, 98.

The authors and publishers acknowledge the following sources of copyright material and are grateful for the permissions granted. While every effort has been made, it has not always been possible to identify the sources of all the material used, or to trace all copyright holders. If any omissions are brought to our notice, we will be happy to include the appropriate acknowledgements on reprinting.

Contents

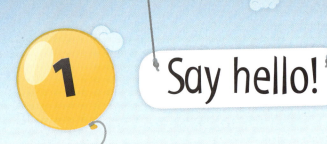

1 Say hello!

A Hello! Say, spell and write names.

My name is ....

What's your name? ....

B ▶ Know your letters!

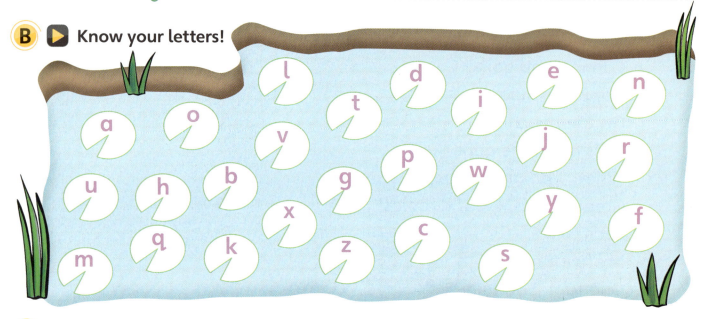

C Draw a **red** line (a–z) from the baby spider to its dad!

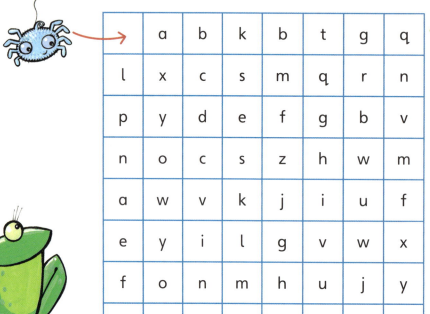

a	b	k	b	t	g	q
l	x	c	s	m	q	r	n
p	y	d	e	f	g	b	v
n	o	c	s	z	h	w	m
a	w	v	k	j	i	u	f
e	y	i	l	g	v	w	x
f	o	n	m	h	u	j	y
x	p	q	r	s	t	k	z

D ▶ Listen! Draw a line from the baby frog to its mum!

E What's this? Write the word.

f h s i ¹ d k c u ² h s e p

Example .... fish ....
1 ....
2 ....

3 ....
4 ....
5 ....

3 o f g r 4 g t a o 5 p i r d s e

F ▶ What's the animal?

1 g o a t
2 _ _ e _ _
3 _ _ i _ _ _
4 _ _ o _
5 _ u _ _

_ a _

_ o _

_ _ a _ e

Do you know these animals too?

This cat's name is ....

This dog's name is ....

This snake's name is ....

G Play the game! Can you make a word?

2 Numbers, numbers, numbers

A Write the numbers.

two ....2....   five ....   seven ....
eight ....   nine ....   ten ....
eleven ....   twelve ....   thirteen ....
fifteen ....   twenty ....

B Look at the letters. Write words for six things in the picture.

r c a

c a r

1 d b e

_ _ _

2 o s k c

_ _ _ _

3 e s h o

_ _ _ _

4 k o b o

_ _ _ _

5 t a c

_ _ _

6

_ _ _ _ _ _ _

C What can you see in the picture? Answer the questions.

How many cats are there in the picture?   ....3....
How many balls are there?   ....
How many shoes are there?   ....

8

D ▶ Listen! Write a name or number.

What's the boy's name?	.... *Tom* ....
How old is he?	.... *9* ....
1 How many toys has Tom got?	....
2 What's the name of Tom's cat?	....
3 How many books has Tom got?	....
4 What the name of Tom's school?	.... School
5 Which class is Tom in?	....

E Listen and draw lines between the letters and numbers.

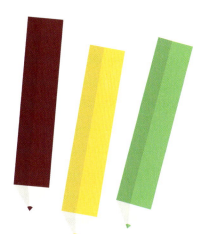

F Colour and draw.

Colour **B** brown. Colour **G** green.
And draw a big yellow sun in the picture!

G Play number games!

3 What's your name?

A Look at the letters. Write the names.

1 n e B
  <u>B e n</u>

2 s m a
  _ _ _

3 c L u y
  _ _ _ _

4 k i N c
  _ _ _ _

5 B l i l
  _ _ _ _

6 n A n
  _ _ _

7 o m T
  _ _ _

8 i m K
  _ _ _

9

B Write the names under *boy*, *girl* or *boy and girl*.

~~Dan~~ Alex Sue Tony
Anna Jill May Pat Grace

Dan ....

....
....
....
....
....
....
....

My favourite English names are:

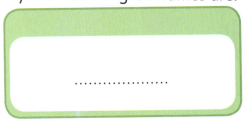
....

and

....

C ▶ Listen and write the names.

1 .... Tom ....   3 Mr ....   5 ....
2 ....   4 ....   6 Mrs ....

10

D **Answer the questions. Write your names in the circle.**

1   What's your name?
2   What's your friend's name?
3   What's your grandmother's name?
4   What's a good name for a cat or a dog?

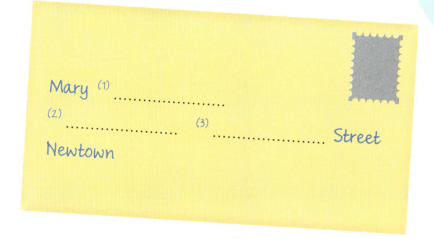

E ▶ **Listen and write the names and numbers.**

Mary (1) ....
(2) .... (3) .... Street
Newtown

F **It's your friend's birthday!**
Write your friend's name and address.

....
....
....

G **Find a name from A in these sentences.**

1   Listen to my story!
2   I like the cat on your bag.
3   She wants an orange and an apple.

4   Grandma, you're great!
5   My face is clean now.
6   Stop at the end of the street.

H **Play the game! Names bingo.**

4 Red, blue and yellow

A Read and colour.

1 blue + red = ...
2 white + black = ...
3 blue + yellow = ...
4 yellow + red = ...
5 red + white = ...

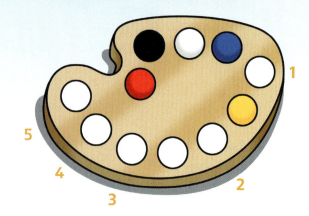

B You and colours. Answer the questions.

What colour are your eyes?

What colour is your T-shirt?

What colour is your bedroom?

What colour is your hair?

What is your favourite colour?

C Look at the pictures. Circle the correct word.

1 This is a boat / goat.
2 This is a cat / mat.
3 This is a kite / tree.
4 This is a boy / woman.

D ▶ Listen and colour the birds.

E Great colours for a car, sports shoes, ice cream or bike!

What's a good colour for a ?   What colour do you like?

What colour are your favourite ?   What's a great colour for a  ?

What colour is your favourite ?

5 Answering questions

A Complete the crossword. Find the answers in the box.

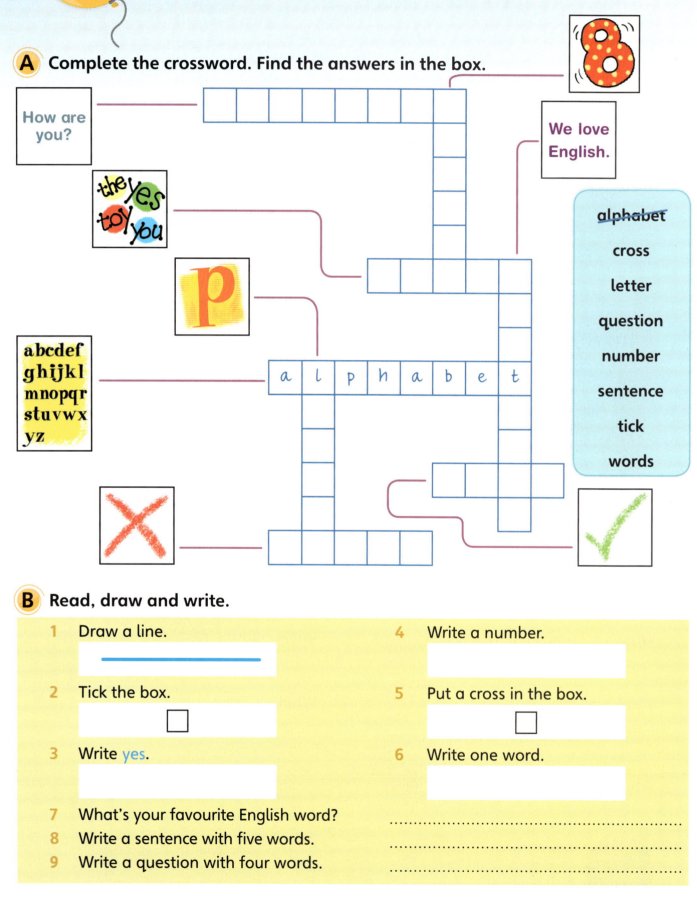

How are you?

We love English.

the yes toy you

abcdef ghijkl mnopqr stuvwx yz

| a | l | p | h | a | b | e | t |

alphabet

cross

letter

question

number

sentence

tick

words

B Read, draw and write.

1   Draw a line.

2   Tick the box.

3   Write yes.

4   Write a number.

5   Put a cross in the box.

6   Write one word.

7   What's your favourite English word?   ....

8   Write a sentence with five words.   ....

9   Write a question with four words.   ....

14

C Look and read. Write yes or no.

Examples

The dog is playing with a ball.	..........yes..........
There are six apples on the tree.	..........no..........

Questions

1   The girl has got black hair.   ....

2   You can see two books.   ....

3   The children are in the house.   ....

4   The boy is wearing a blue T-shirt.   ....

5   The frog is between the two children.   ....

D ▶ Listen and draw lines.

E Mime the sentence.

6 Animals and aliens

A Look and read. Put a tick (✔) or a cross (✗) in the box.

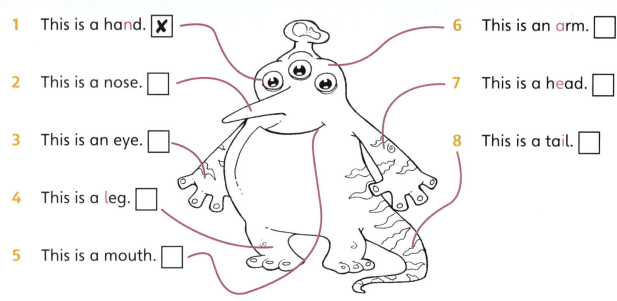

1   This is a hand. [✗]

2   This is a nose. [ ]

3   This is an eye. [ ]

4   This is a leg. [ ]

5   This is a mouth. [ ]

6   This is an arm. [ ]

7   This is a head. [ ]

8   This is a tail. [ ]

9   This is an _ _ _ _ _ _ !

B Write the animals, then draw lines from *a* or *an*.

a

an

arm

body

ear

eye

face

foot

hand

head

leg

mouth

nose

tail

....

....

16

C **Read and choose a word from the box.**
Write the correct word next to numbers 1–5.

You can find me at the ....zoo.......... . I'm a very big
(1) .... I've got four long (2) .... and
my tail is very long too. I can see with my big brown
(3) .... I like eating (4) .... , but
I don't eat meat. I drink (5) ....
My body is yellow, orange and brown.
What am I? I am a giraffe.

Example

zoo	water	legs	animal
fruit	shoe	eyes	nose

D **Write about this animal now.**

I'm .... and I'm a very .... animal.
I can run with my .... legs and I have
a ....
I like eating .... but I don't eat meat.
I drink .... and I love swimming in it too!
What am I?
I'm a _ _ _ _ _

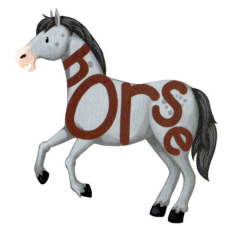

E **Play two games!**

Make the animals!

Have you got the lizard's tail?

7 'Look, listen, smile, draw'

A Look at the pictures. Look at the letters. Write the words.

Example e a r

1 _ _ _ _   e f c a

2 _ _ _ _   d a h n

3 _ _ _ _   o e s n

4 _ _ _ _   t e e f

5 _ _ _ _ _   o h u t m

B What's not there? Write the parts of the face.

1 his ..ears.. 2 her .... 3 his .... 4 his .... 5 her ....

C Choose and write the correct word.

1 I .... with my mouth.
2 I .... and .... with my eyes.
3 I .... to music with my ears.
4 I .... at my friends with my hand.
5 I can .... a ball with my feet and I can ....
   with my feet and legs.

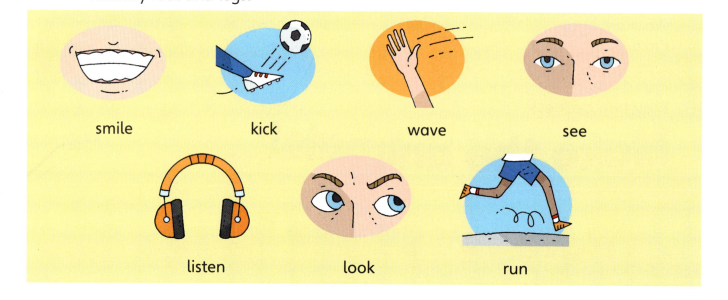

smile   kick   wave   see

listen   look   run

D Look at Sam's robot. Choose and write words on the lines.

computer   clock   keyboard   kites   socks

1   The ....*computer*.... is the robot's face.
2   The .... is the robot's mouth.
3   The .... is the robot's body.
4   The .... are the robot's arms.
5   The .... are the robot's legs.

Now draw the robot's eyes, ears and nose.

E Look at the picture. Find words to complete the sentences.

The family are
....*smiling*........ . But they
aren't sitting on chairs! The
boy's (1) .... from
the tree! Can you see the
(2) .... under his
sister? The old man and
woman are sitting on two
(3) .... The
baby's got a flower in her
(4) .... and she and
her mum are sitting on a big
(5) .... The cat's
on the shoe! Can you see its
brown (6) .... ?

smiling   frog   tail   hand
boxes   ball   waving

F Play the game! Draw the monkey.

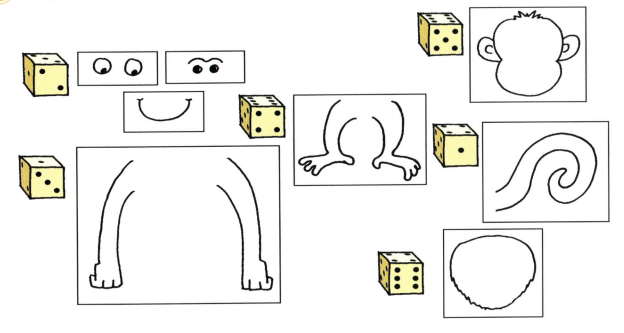

8 In my clothes cupboard

A Write the words for the pictures.

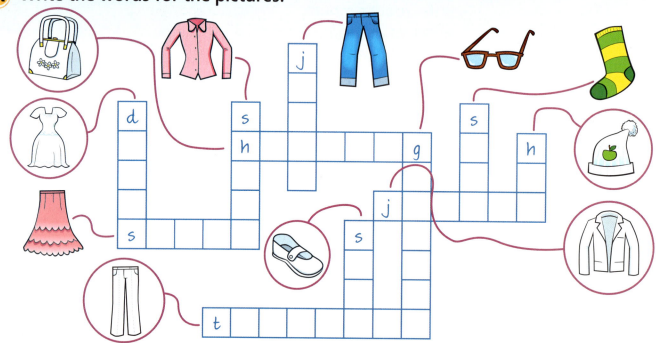

B ▶ Listen and tick (✔) the box.

1 Which boy is Tom?

A ☐   B ☐   C ☐

2 Which is Kim's dad?

A ☐   B ☐   C ☐

3 Which woman is Dan's teacher?

A ☐   B ☐   C ☐

4 Where's the T-shirt?

A ☐   B ☐   C ☐

C Look at the picture. Write one-word answers to the questions.

Examples

What colour is the boy's T-shirt?   red ....

How many sofas are there?   1 ....

1   Where's the jacket?   on the ....

2   How many people are there in the picture?   ....

3   What colour is the woman's skirt?   ....

4   What's the baby wearing on one of her feet?   a blue ....

5   What colour is the girl's hair?   ....

D Make sentences.

1 | four | There are | green | chairs |

....

2 | white | There are | two | lamps |

....

3 | baby | There is | one | happy |

....

4 | .... | .... | cats | .... |

....

5 | .... | .... | .... | flowers |

....

E Play the game! The long clothes sentence.

9 Funny monsters

A Look, read and write numbers. Then, draw and colour the clothes.

The monster

I've got ....2........... heads and .... eyes. I've got .... noses. I haven't got a mouth, but I've got .... funny tails.

My .... feet are very big. My .... arms are very long and my hands are very small.

Today I'm wearing hats and socks and a big T-shirt.

B Read and colour the monster.

1 The monster's arms are red and its hands are green.
2 It's got purple faces, pink eyes and yellow noses.
3 Colour three socks blue and two socks orange.
4 Make its T-shirt pink and its hats orange.

C Choose words and write about the monster!

Say 'Hello' to Bounce!
It's very big/small, happy/sad, very beautiful/ugly, and funny!
It drinks .... and .... is its favourite food!

22

D Who am I? Look at the pictures. Write the number of the monster.

1 I've got a flower in my hair.   monster ....4........
2 I'm holding my baby.   monster ....
3 I love reading funny stories.   monster ....
4 I've got my robot in my hand.   monster ....
5 I really like my new glasses!   monster ....

The monster picture hall

....

E Look at the monsters. Write colours.

Monster	body	hair	eyes	nose	arms	feet
1	blue	black	red	blue	0	red
2						
3						
4						

F Write names for monsters 1–3 under the pictures in the Picture Hall.

G Listen and complete the sentences about monster 5.

Hi! My name's .... I love reading
.... stories and learning about ....
in the .... at my new school.

H ▶ Play the game! Colour the wall.

What's that?

It's a funny monster!

10 Our families

A Read about Sam. Which picture is Sam's family?

My name's Sam. I live in a big house with my (mum) and dad and my three sisters and two brothers. My grandpa and grandma live in the small blue house next to us. We all love animals. We've got a dog. His name's Chocolate and he plays and sleeps in our garden. My grandparents have got a cat and three fish. The cat's name is Lucy but I don't know the names of their fish!

1

2

3

B Put circles round the family words.

C Complete the sentences about Sam's family's pets.

1 This is our ....

2 These are our ....

3 This is my ....

my favourite ....

D **Answer the questions.**

1   Is your street long or short? ....
2   How many people live in your house/flat? ....
3   Do your grandfathers and grandmothers live with you? ....
4   Have you got a lot of cousins? ....
5   Has your family got a pet? ....

E **Draw circles round words about your family and home and write names.**

My name's ....

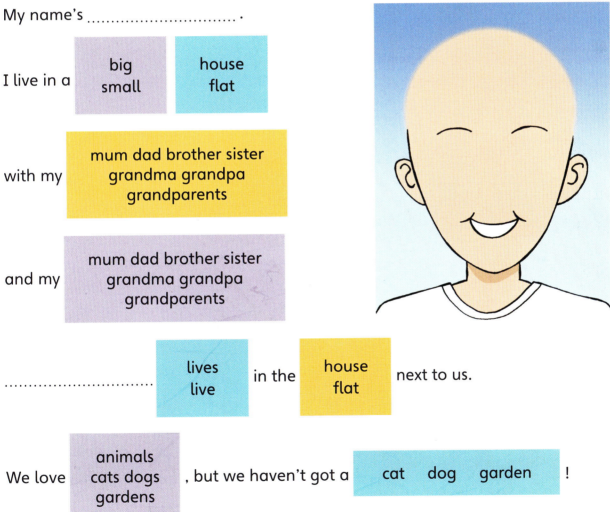

I live in a | big small | house flat

with my | mum dad brother sister grandma grandpa grandparents

and my | mum dad brother sister grandma grandpa grandparents

.... | lives live | in the | house flat | next to us.

We love | animals cats dogs gardens | , but we haven't got a | cat   dog   garden | !

F **Play the game! Who's that?**

11 'Whose is it?'

A Look and read. Put a tick (✔) or a cross (✘) in the box.

Examples

 This is a lizard. ✔

 This is an eye. ✘

Questions

1 This is a robot. ☐

4 This is a cake. ☐

2 This is a sock. ☐

5 This is a keyboard. ☐

3 This is a name. ☐

B Look, read and write answers.

1	Whose mouse is it?	It's Nick's.	It's his.
2	Whose watch is it?	It's	It's hers.
3	Whose tennis ball is it?	It's	It's
4	Whose clock is it?	It's	It's
5	Whose kite is it?	It's	It's
6	Whose paints are they?	They're	They're

C ▶ Listen and draw lines.

D Are they his or hers?

Bill has got five things in this cupboard. His favourite colour is red. Bill likes taking photos and drawing.

Jill has got four things. She likes music, doing sport and going to the beach.

The .... , ... , ... ,
.... and the .... are Bill's things.
The .... , ... , ... and the
.... are Jill's things.

E Play the games! What have you got?

12 'Who's got the red balloon?'

A Find the words and write them on the lines under the picture.

womenrlgirliababyprowomantboyrotmangbochildrenmen

Park

b _ _ _   b _ _   g _ _ _   c _ _ _ _ _ _ _ _

m _ _   m _ _   w _ _ _ _   w _ _ _ _ _

B Write **yes** or **no**.

Examples

Two girls have got a duck.   ...yes...   The men have got a ball.   ...no...

Questions

1	A boy has got a kite.	....	7	Two men have got a duck.	....
2	A man has got a horse.	....	8	A boy has got a book.	....
3	A woman has got a book.	....	9	A woman has got a handbag.	....
4	A girl has got an ice cream.	....			
5	A baby has got a horse.	....	10	Two women have got some flowers.	....
6	A man has got a dog.	....			

C Ask and answer questions about people.

Is your best friend a boy or a girl?

a ....

Is your English teacher a man or a woman?

a ....

How many people are there in your family?

....

How many children are there in your class?

....

D Look at the pictures and answer the questions.

Examples:

How many children are there?
................2................

What's the boy watching?
the ....television....

1   What's the girl doing?
....

2   What does the boy want?
his ....

3   Where's the girl looking?
behind the ....

4   Where are the children now?
in the ....

5   Who's got the phone?
the ....

E Play the game! Nine lives.

13 'Who can do this?'

A Five funny monsters! Look at the ticks (✔) and crosses (✗).

	fly	swim	read	jump	run	sing
Alphabet	✔	✗	✗	✔	✔	✗
Bean	✗	✗	✗	✗	✗	✔
Carrot	✗	✗	✔	✔	✔	✔
Doll						
Egg	✗	✔	✗	✗	✗	✗

Which monster? Write the names.

1 He can sing but he can't run, read, fly, swim or jump. ....
2 She can jump, run, sing and read but she can't fly or swim ....
3 He can't fly or read or jump or run or sing but he can swim! ....

B Listen and tick (✔) the box.

What is Egg doing now?

A ☐   B ☐   C ☐

1 Where is Doll?

A ☐   B ☐   C ☐

2 Where is Bean singing?

A ☐   B ☐   C ☐

3 What is Carrot reading about?

A ☐   B ☐   C ☐

4 What can Egg's baby brother do?

A ☐   B ☐   C ☐

5 What can Alphabet draw?

A ☐   B ☐   C ☐

30

C **Read about me and my classmates. Write our names.**

Alex has got a really big garden. He can play badminton with his dad there.

Lucy can ride a horse. She's really good at riding horses.

I love Anna's paintings. They're great! She draws beautiful pictures!

Nick likes riding his bike. He can ride his bike to school.

Dan has got a new camera. He can take really good photos.

My name's May. I can play the guitar very well. Can you see my guitar?

Bill's good at singing. He writes funny songs and sings them in class!

Grace loves fishing. She's got a boat and catches lots of fish in the sea.

Kim can play tennis. She likes playing tennis with her big sister.

Mr Page is our teacher. He's really good at swimming. We can have a swimming lesson now!

1 ......Kim........ 2 .... 3 ....

4 .... 5 .... 6 ....

7 .... 8 .... 9 ....

10 ....

D **Play the game! Stand up. Sit down again.**

PROJECT

31

14 Big, small, happy or sad?

A Look and answer the questions.

1 What's this?   a _ _ _ _ _ _ _ _ _
2 Have you got a ....?
3 Is this .... big or small?

1 What are these?   _ _ _ _ _ _
2 Are you wearing .... today?
3 Are these .... long or short?

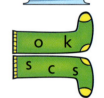

1 What's this?   a _ _ _ _ _ _
2 What colour is this ....?
3 Is this .... old or new?

1 What are these?   _ _ _ _ _ _ _ _ _ _
2 Do you wear .... to school?
3 Are these .... clean or dirty?

B Write the word under the picture.

beautiful   young   ugly   old   short   ~~clean~~   long   dirty   old   new

1

a ...clean... car

2
a .... car

3
an .... shoe

4
a .... shoe

5
a .... woman

6
an .... woman

7

a .... spider

8

an .... spider

9

a .... skirt

10
a .... skirt

C Choose words and draw pictures.

A	big	boy	is drawing a	red	snake.
	sad	girl	is painting a	blue	computer.
	funny	horse	is holding a	yellow	kite.
	small	cat	is playing with a	black	fish.
	happy	elephant	is riding a	green	alien.
	short	mouse	is watching a	white	balloon.

D Look and read. Write yes or no.

Anna   Lucy   Tony   Pat

Examples

The small dog is happy.	...yes....
The big ball is in the dog's mouth.	.....no.....
1 The girl in the blue dress is sad.	....
2 One boy is wearing red shoes.	....
3 One of the girls is eating an ice cream.	....
4 The boy with dirty hands is smiling.	....
5 These children are in a house.	....

E Read, write and draw lines.

1   Pat's wearing ......jeans........ and a blue and white T-shirt.

2   Anna's got long brown .... She's wearing a blue dress. She's sad today.

3   Lucy's got a chocolate ice cream. She's wearing ....

4   Tony's playing with Pat. Tony's wearing ....

F Play the game! Opposites bingo.

15 One, two, three animals

A Match animal numbers and animal words.

1

5 chicken .... small, brown, walk ....

mouse ....

2

snake ....

frog ....

3

hippo ....

giraffe ....

4

spider ....

sheep ....

5

fish ....

cow ....

6

crocodile ....

tiger ....

7

elephant ....

lizard ....

8

goat ....

9

10

11

12

13

14

15

B Write words next to the animals.

big	black	grey	red	fly
long	blue	orange	white	jump
beautiful	brown	pink	yellow	run
short	green	purple		swim
ugly				walk
small				

C What am I? Choose an animal and complete the sentences.

I'm .... and I'm .... I've got .... legs.

I can .... but I can't ....

D Where are Tom's pets? Draw lines.

1	in the box
2	on the ball
3	in the shoe
4	under the kite
5	on the hat
6	in the water

E Talk about the picture.

Where's?   What's?   How many?   What colour?   What's he / she / it doing?

F Play the game! At the zoo.

16 What's your favourite fruit?

A Look at the pictures. Write the words.

| apple (crossed out) |
| banana |
| beans |
| carrot |
| coconut |
| grapes |
| lemon |
| lime |
| mango |
| onion |
| orange |
| pea |
| pear |
| pineapple |
| potato |
| tomato |
| watermelon |

3 across: a p p l e

B What am I?

1   I'm a fruit. I'm long and yellow. Monkeys like me.   I'm a ..... *banana* ..... .
2   I'm very small and green, but I'm not a bean.   I'm a ....
3   I'm brown and white. There's lots of milk in me.   I'm a ....
4   I'm yellow. You can make a great drink from me.   I'm a ....
5   I'm a fruit and a colour. You can make fruit juice from me. I'm an ....
6   I'm red and round. Some people put me on pizzas.   I'm a ....
7   I'm long and orange and horses love eating me.   I'm a ....

C Spell and say *tomatoes* and *potatoes!*

_ _ _ _

_ _ _ _

_ _ _ _

t o m a _ _ _ _ _

p o t a _ _ _ _

D ▶ What's in Ben's funny fruit drink?

Tick (✔) four boxes.

pear	☐
tomato	☐
carrot	☐
orange	☐
pineapple	☐
grapes	☐
mango	☐
banana	☐
lemon	☐

What's in your drink?

.... , ... , ... , ... and ....!

E Talk about the picture.

1 Where's the coconut?
2 Where are the lizards?
3 What's this?

4 What colour is the .... ?
5 How many .... are there?
6 What's the bird doing?

F Play the game! Say it three times.

What's on the menu?

A Write the menu. Add your favourite lunch to the menu, too!

Today's Menu

For lunch, try our
- burger and chips
- ....
- ....
- ....
- ....
- ....

onions

potatoes

sausages

chicken

fish

rice

tomatoes

eggs

B Write the drinks.

w t a r e
_ _ _ _ _

c i j u e
_ _ _ _ _

m k i l
_ _ _ _

d m e o l n a e
_ _ _ _ _ _ _ _

h l o a c c t e o
hot _ _ _ _ _ _ _ _ _

C ▶ **Listen and tick (✔) Lucy's lunch and Tony's lunch.**

Today's Menu

fish	tomatoes	
chicken	peas	ice cream
eggs	beans	fruit
sausages	carrots	
	potatoes	

D **Write Tony's lunch.**

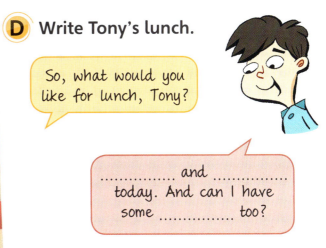

So, what would you like for lunch, Tony?

.... and ....
today. And can I have
some .... too?

E **What would you like for lunch? Write your words.**

Now, what would you like for lunch?

.... and ....
today. And can I have
some .... too?

F **Talk about the kitchen picture.**

G ▶ **Listen and draw lines.**

8 'A colourful house'

A Look at the house. What colour are these rooms?

> bedroom   bathroom   hall   dining room   living room   kitchen

B ▶ Listen and draw lines.

1 clock
2 ....
3 ....
4 ....
5 ....
6 ....
7 ....

C Look, read and write one-word answers about the house.

1 Where's the photo?   In the .... *hall* ....
2 Where's the mat?   In the ....
3 Where's the clock?   In the ....
4 Where's the lamp?   In the ....
5 Where's the mirror?   In the ....

D Read and write! Which home words can you see in the mirrors?

Example ....wall.......

1 ....

2 ....

3 ....

4 ....

5 ....

E Read this. Choose a word from the box. Write the correct word next to numbers 1–5.

A desk

I'm white and I've got four ......legs......, but I'm not an animal like a (1) ...horse... or a goat. I'm in front of the window in Lucy's (2) ...bedroom.... Lucy sits on a grey (3) ...chair... next to me. She puts her favourite (4) ...stories... on me and reads them. Lucy puts her (5) ...computer... on me too and plays games on it. What am I? I am a desk.

Example

legs   computer   chair   stories

bedroom   ear   horse   water

F Write about your home.

My house is in (1) .... It's got (2) .... rooms.

There are: (3) ....

My favourite room is (4) ....

In my favourite room, you can find (5) ....

....

G Play the game! The long home sentence.

PROJECT

19 'What's in your bedroom?'

A What can you see in the room? Write the words next to the numbers.

1 a <u>r m c h a i r</u>
2 b _ _ _ _ _ _ _ _
3 c _ _ _ _ _
4 c _ _ _ _ _ _ _ _
5 d _ _ _
6 d _ _ _ _ _
7 p _ _ _ _ _
8 p _ _ _ _ _
9 p _ _ _ _ _ _ _
10 t _ _ _ _ _ _ _ _ _ _ _
11 w _ _ _ _
12 w _ _ _ _ _ _

B ▶ Listen and colour.

C What's in your bedroom?

In my bedroom, there's a ....,
a .... , a ....
and a ....

42

D Make, write and say two home words!

2×2=

cup   board

c _ _ _ _ _ _ _ _ _

a

and an

a _ _ _ _ _ _ _ _

cupboard

arm   chair

armchair

E Nick loves fish. Write **Nick** on the line under his bedroom. Then, complete the sentences about his bedroom.

..........................'s room

..........................'s room

In Nick's bedroom:

1   the mat is ....*orange*........ .

2   the .... is yellow.

3   the .... is red.

4   the walls are ....

5   the .... is blue.

6   the bookcase is ....

7   the .... is big but in Anna's room it's small.

F ▶ Listen and answer questions about Nick.

1   ....
2   ....
3   ....

4   ....
5   ....
6   ....

G Play the game! Guess what I'm drawing.

20 Alex, Ben and Kim live here!

A Look and read. Put a tick (✔) or a cross (✘) in the box.

Examples

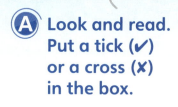

This is a bed. ✔

This is a mouse. ✘

1 This is a kitchen. ☐

2 This is a camera. ☐

This is a family. ☐

4 This is a chair. ☐

5 This is a cat. ☐

B Write the correct word next to numbers 1–5.

A living room

I am in a ......*house*...... or flat. Kim's (1) ....
sit in me in the big (2) .... or on the sofa.
Kim and her brother like watching (3)....................... in me.
There is a (4) .... of Kim's dog on my wall.
The room next to me is the (5) ....,
What am I? I am a living room.

family **television** **photo** **bed** **armchairs** **house** **kitchen**

C Write names and numbers. You choose!

1 The family live in .... Street.

2 The number of their house is ....

3 The boy's name is .... and the girl's name is ....

4 .... animals live with this family.

D ▶ **Listen and colour Ben's street.**

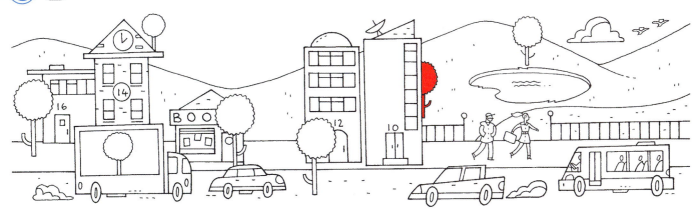

E **Read the sentences. Write Ben or Kim.**

1 In ....'s street, many houses are small.

2 There are no cars or lorries in ....'s street.

3 There's a bookshop in ....'s street.

4 In ....'s street, the flats are very tall.

5 There's a park behind ....'s street.

6 There are no trees in ....'s street.

7 You can see lots of people in ....'s street.

F **Write five questions!**

Is your garden big or small? ....

....

....

....

....

21 'Play with us!'

A Who's playing with the toys? Listen and write names.

Ann
Bill
Dan
Kim
May
Pat
Grace
Jill
Sam
Tony

B You can't ride on or in one of these things. Cross it out!

1	boat	train	~~bean~~
2	bus	box	motorbike
3	plane	bike	phone
4	hat	helicopter	car
5	lorry	hobby	truck

C What am I?

I go on the

c	a	r

I go in the

I go on the

And I go on the

D ▶ Listen and tick (✔) the box.

Example What is Sam riding?

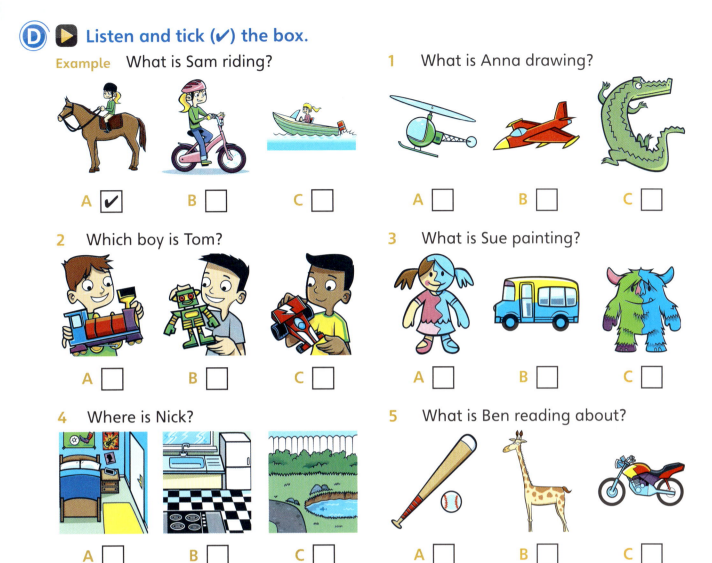

A ✔ B ☐ C ☐

1 What is Anna drawing?

A ☐ B ☐ C ☐

2 Which boy is Tom?

A ☐ B ☐ C ☐

3 What is Sue painting?

A ☐ B ☐ C ☐

4 Where is Nick?

A ☐ B ☐ C ☐

5 What is Ben reading about?

A ☐ B ☐ C ☐

E Talk about your ride on your flying bike!

Would you like to ride a flying bike?
Sit on it now and fly!
What can you see?
Where are you going?

F Play the game! Let's make a helicopter crossword.

22 In our bags and in our school

A How many school words can you find?

b o o k c a s e c u p b o a r d d e s k f l o o r
p i c t u r e t e a c h e r r u l e r e r a s e r
w a l l b a g c o m p u t e r p e n c i l
k e y b o a r d p a g e m o u s e
r u b b e r w i n d o w

B Write the words for the pictures. Which word can you see in the blue box?

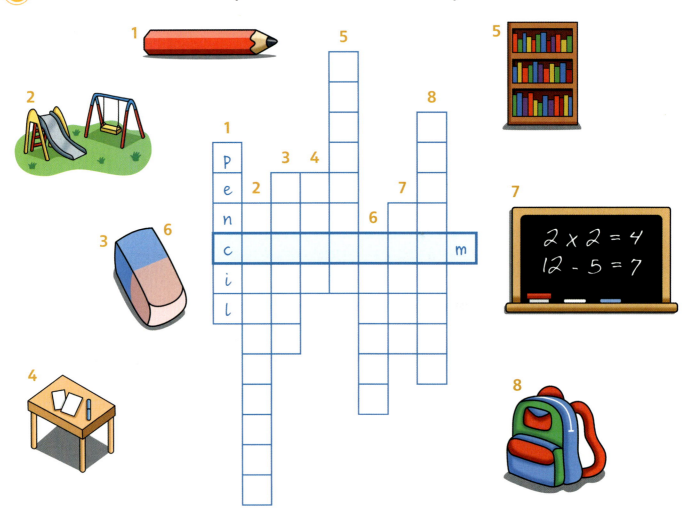

C Write names. Ask your friends and write their answers.

Name:

....

....

....

....

1 So, what colour is your eraser? ....

2 How many pens have you got? ....

3 What's on your desk? ....

4 Do you like your school playground? ....

D Read this. Choose a word from the box. Write the correct word next to numbers 1–5.

Pat's bag

Pat's reading a new ....book........ . He's taking that to school in me today.
Pat writes with his [1] .... and pencils. Those are in me too. And he has a [2] .... He draws lines with that.
He's taking an [3] .... to eat to school today, and some [4] .... That's his favourite drink!
Pat wears [5] .... at school. Those are in me too. What am I? I am a bag.

Example

book   glasses   juice   shirt

apple   ruler   pens   shells

E Answer questions about Alex's bag.

1 What fruit does Alex have in his bag?
an apple and a ....

2 How many pencils can you see?
....

3 What colour is the ruler?
....

4 What can you see behind the apple?
a ....

5 Where is the bag?
on the ....

6 What drink can you see?
some ....

F Play the game! Close your eyes and draw!

'At our school'

A Write letters on the lines to complete the words.

_ _ _ _ _ case

_ _ _ _ _ _ _ case

_ _ _ _ _ _ _ case

_ _ _ board

_ _ _ board

_ _ _ _ _ board

B Whose is it? Write his, her or their.

1

2

3

It's .... bag.　　It's .... ruler.　　It's .... dog.

C ▶ Read the question. Listen and write a name or a number.

Examples

How old is May?　　　　　　　　　　　　　　　　　　　　　　 8

What is May's brother's name?　　　　　　　　　　　　　 Nick

1　Where is May's school?　　　　　　　　　　　　　 .... Street

2　How many children are there in May's class?　 ....

3　What is the name of May's friend?　　　　　 ....

4　Who is May's English teacher?　　　　　　　 Mrs ....

5　What is the number of May's class?　　　　　 ....

D Read about Grace's school and complete the questions.

> Hello! I go to Clock School. It's in Watch Street. I'm in class ten now. There are 25 children in my class. My new teacher is Miss Hall. She's very nice. My friend Dan sits next to me.

1 What's the name of your .... ?
2 Where's your .... ?
3 Which .... are you in?
4 How many .... are there in your class?
5 What's your .... 's name?
6 Who do you .... next to?

E Answer the questions from E about *your* school.

Our school

I go to .... school.
My school is in ....
I am in class ....
There are .... students in my class. Our English teacher's name is ....
I sit next to ....

F What am I? Read and write yes or no next to the words.

1 I am in a house or classroom.
   a beach ..no..   a flower ....   a bookcase ....   a computer ....
   a rubber ....   a pencil ....   a chicken ....   a door ....

2 I am on a table.
   a flower ....   a bookcase ....   a computer ....   a rubber ....
   a pencil ....   a door ....

3 People write, draw and play with me.
   a flower ....   a computer ....   a rubber ....   a pencil ....

4 I have lots of letters and numbers on my keyboard.
   a computer ....   a pencil ....

What am I?   I'm a __ __ __ __ __ __ __ __ !

24 What's the class doing?

A Listen and answer.

1

2

B Are you looking at picture 1 or picture 2?

1 The teacher is reading a story. ....1.........

2 A boy is eating a banana. ....

3 One girl is jumping. ....

4 The children are sitting down. ....

5 One girl is painting. ....

6 The children are listening to the teacher. ....

7 A boy is sleeping on his desk. ....

8 Two boys are drawing on the board. ....

C Listen to the questions and write one-word answers about picture 2.

What are Tom and Nick doing?

.....drawing.....

What are they drawing?

a .....rocket.....

1 a ....

2 on his ....

3 a ....

4 a ....

D Put the words in the cupboard.

read run smile stop draw swim wave ride sleep

E What are you doing?
I'm doing a crossword.

s
m
i
l
i
n
g

i   e   g

r
e   i

i   g

w

r   n

F What are the children doing now?

G Play the game! Action mimes.

A Which animals can you see in the picture?
Can you find ten animals?

B ▶ **Listen and colour the snakes.**

C What can you see in the animal picture? Put a tick (✔) or a cross (✗) in the box.

D ▶ Listen and write.

	Our guesses
Tom's got three	....
They live in his	....
Tom likes .... with them.	....
Their names are Lucy, Ben and	....
They eat Tom's mum's ....!	....

E Read the sentences and write animal word answers.

Example

I'm green or brown. You can find me in
and next to water.   a c _ _ _ _ _ _ _ _

1   I'm grey and my body is very fat. I can swim
    but I can walk too.   a h _ _ _ _ _

2   I live in trees. I eat bananas. I've got a tail.   a m _ _ _ _ _ _

3   I'm long. I eat meat. I haven't got legs.   a s _ _ _ _ _

4   I'm small and long. I eat insects. I can run.   a l _ _ _ _ _ _

5   I'm small. I can fly. I eat plants and small animals.
    I can sing.   a b _ _ _

6   I'm very small but I've got a long tail. I can run. a m _ _ _ _ _

7   I catch insects and eat them. I've got eight legs. a s _ _ _ _ _ _

8   I've got four legs and my body is white (or black!).
    I say Baa!   a s _ _ _ _ _

9   I don't have legs but I've got a tail. I can swim. a f _ _ _ _

10 I like meat. I'm orange and black and I've got a tail. a t _ _ _ _ _

11 I've got four legs and I eat grass. You can get milk from me. a c _ _

12 I eat spiders and flies. I live next to the water. I can jump! a f _ _ _ _

F Project! Where do animals live?

26 How many pets?

A ▶ **Listen and write a name or a number.**

Examples

What's the girl's name?   May .... *Read* ....   How old is she? .... 10 ....

1   How many pets has she got?   ....

2   What's her dog's name?   ....

3   How many mice does she have?   ....

4   What's the name of her favourite pet?   Mr ....

5   How old is the crocodile?   ....

B **Complete the man's questions.**

1   How many .... have you got?

2   How many .... do you have?

3   How many .... have you got?

4   How many .... do you have?

1

3

5

18

C **Let's talk about your pets!**

How many .... have you got / do you have?

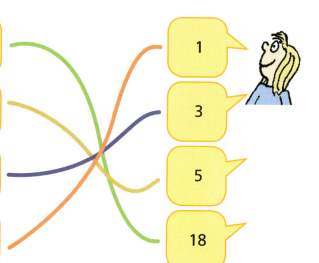

How many pets have you got?

Which pets would you like to have?

D Write the words in the *one* or *two* bag.

dress beaches
toys story cross
mats babies
body buses family
day tails sausage
tree names

E Look and read. Write yes or no.

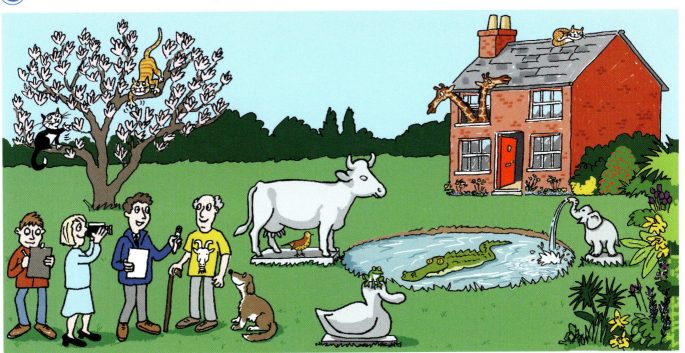

Examples

You can see a goat on the man's T-shirt. ....yes.............

The door of the house is closed. ....no.................

1   A frog is sitting on the dog's head. ....

2   There are two giraffes in the window. ....

3   One cat is sleeping in the tree. ....

4   You can see a crocodile in the water. ....

5   A bird is under the cow. ....

27 'Food I really like!'

A Bill's big breakfast.

sweets

egg food

juice bread

peas fruit

breakfast

beans

B Write six things that Lucy likes for lunch.
Lucy likes food which has the letter 'c' in it.

....

....

....

....

....

....

C Dan's funny dinner. Look at the letters. Write the words.

g s
e g

r g r
e b u

e g g s

_ _ _ _ _ _

d e r
b a

t o o t e
p a s

_ _ _ _ _ _

_ _ _ _ _ _

a l e
s p p

p p i e l
e e l
a n p

_ _ _ _ _ _

_ _ _ _ _ _

D ▶ Listen and tick (✔) the box.

Example What can Kim have for lunch?

A ☐   B ☐   C ✔

1 What is May's favourite meat?

A ☐   B ☐   C ☐

2 What does Alex want for breakfast today?

A ☐   B ☐   C ☐

3 What can Tony have for supper?

A ☐   B ☐   C ☐

4 Which drink does Ann like?

A ☐   B ☐   C ☐

5 Which is Sue's favourite ice cream?

A ☐   B ☐   C ☐

E Listen and write the food and drink.

I like ... 🙂	I don't like ... 🙁	I don't know ... 😐

F Play lots of games with food!

28 My favourite food day

A Write your answers.

Me

My favourite food is ① ....

I don't like ② .... or ....

For breakfast I eat ③ .... and ....

For lunch I drink ④ ....

For dinner I eat ⑤ ....

My favourite ice cream is ⑥ .... ice cream.

B Read the questions. Put the correct answer numbers in the yellow circles.

What's your favourite ice cream? (6)

What do you eat for breakfast? ( )

What do you drink for lunch? ( )

What's your favourite food? ( )

What do you eat for dinner? ( )

What food don't you like? ( )

C Write your friend's answers.

Name: ....

....

....

....

....

....

....

D Write your menu.

My favourite food day

breakfast	lunch	dinner
....	....	....
....	....	....
....	....	....
....	....	....

E Spell and say *onions* and *sausages*!

on i on s

onions

sa u sa ges

sausages

Anna puts one onion under Sue's seven sausages!

F Read this. Choose a word from the box. Write the correct word next to numbers 1–5.

An apple

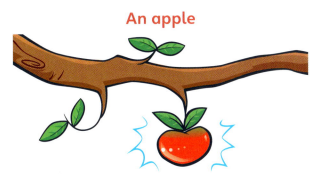

I'm a .... *fruit* .... but I'm not an (1) .... or a pear. I'm

in the tree in Alex's (2) .... People like eating me and

(3) .... like eating me too. Alex likes drinking my (4) ....

My (5) .... are red and green. What am I? I'm an apple!

Example

fruit   colours   breakfast   juice

orange   birds   garden   face

G Play the game! Food, names and animals.

61

29 'We're in the toy shop today'

A Look at the pictures and read the questions. Write one-word answers.

Examples

How many toys are in the big cupboard?   .... 12 ....

What is the man cleaning?   the .... floor ....

1 Which toy is the woman holding?   a ....

2 How many people are in the shop now?   ....

3 What are two of the children sitting on?   a ....

4 Where are the toys now?   on the ....

5 What is the man in the shop doing?   ....

B Ask and answer questions about the toys.

C Look at the third story picture and read. Write **yes** or **no**.

Examples

The women are waving. ....*yes*.........   Three people are in the shop. ....*no*..........

1 The horse is on the car. ....
2 The man is sitting on a chair. ....
3 You can see a clock on the wall. ....
4 There are lots of toys in the cupboard. ....
5 The white cat is sleeping in the street. ....

D Write the words in the boxes.

h	e	l	i	c	o	p	t	e	r

1 What's in the hat?   a ....*boat*........
2 Which toys are red, white and blue?   the .... and the ....
3 What colours are on the doll's dress?   .... and ....
4 How many toys are on the floor?   ....
5 What is standing?   the ....

E Play the game! Stand up and do it, please.

30 Monsters in the park

A Look at the picture. Write sentences about the monsters.

	1	2	3	4	5
A	A	water	in front of	the	behind
B	on	monster	An	tree	under
C	is	green	next to	red	flowers
D	blue	yellow	in	orange	chair

	A1	C2	B2	C1	A5	A4	B4
1	A	green	monster	is	behind	the	tree.
	A1	D1	B2	C1	A3	A4	C5
2	....	....	....	....	....	....	....
	A1	C4	B2	C1	C3	A4	B4
3	....	....	....	....	....	....	....
	B3	D4	B2	C1	D3	A4	A2
4	....	....	....	....	....	....	....
	A1	D2	B2	C1	B1	A4	D5
5	....	....	....	....	....	....	....

B Listen and write the monsters' names.

1   Mr ....

2   Mr ....

3   Miss ....

4   Mrs ....

And the red monster's name? You choose!   Miss/Mrs ....

C In the monster hall.

D Where is it? Choose the right word.

The phone is **on/in** Anna's hand.

The table is **under/on** the mirror.

The monster is **between/behind** Anna.

The chair is **in/between** the table and the door.

The big lamp is **under/next to** the door.

The mat is **in front of/on** the monster.

The books are **behind/next to** the lamp.

E Do the classroom quiz!

Coming and going

A **Look at the picture. Look at the letters. Write the words.**

Example

c a r

1

b e
   i
k

_ _ _ _

2

   p
n e
  l a

_ _ _ _ _

3

   o
l
   y
 r   r

_ _ _ _ _

4

   t o
 r m b
e k i
   o

_ _ _ _ _ _ _ _

5

   r h
   c e
o l
 t p
  e i

_ _ _ _ _ _ _ _ _

B **What does Sue Smile drive, fly or ride?**

Sue Smile drives her	
She flies her	
And she loves riding her	

C **How do you come and go? How would you like to come and go?**

I go to .... by ....

I walk to ....

I'd like to drive / ride / fly a bus / car / helicopter / lorry / motorbike / plane / train.

D **Listen and colour the smiles.**

E Read this. Choose a word from the box.
Write the correct word next to numbers 1–5.

I'm big and long. I'm in the ....street......... .
A woman or a (1) .... drives me. You can
see me between cars, bikes or (2) ....
Many children sit in me. They put their
(3) .... on my floor. I stop next to the
children's (4) .... and next to the school
playground. My (5) .... opens and closes.
What am I? I'm a school bus!

Example

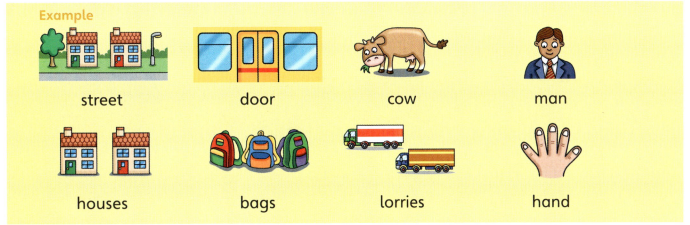

street	door	cow	man
houses	bags	lorries	hand

F Let's talk about the picture.

G What do you have?

I have	a great book		eat.
	a funny game		play.
	a new helicopter	to	read.
	a clean bike		drive.
	a beautiful car		ride.
	some nice sweets		fly.

32 Happy birthday!

A Listen and colour.

B Listen and draw lines.

  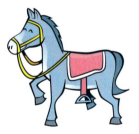

C Answer the questions.

1 What's this?
   It's a ....cake........

2 Do you like cake?
   ....

3 What do you eat for lunch? ....
   ....

1 What's this?
   It's a ....

2 Have you got a jacket?
   ....

3 What clothes are you wearing? ....
   ....

1 What's this?
   It's a ....

2 Can you ride a horse?
   ....

3 What's your favourite animal? ....
   ....

D Look at the picture in A. Read and write the words.

1 You can see food and drink on this.
2 There are four of them. They are standing.
3 The people are in the ....
4 This is behind the people and it's big.

5 This is closed. It's part of the house.
6 One boy has a balloon in his ....
7 There are two of them. They are standing.
8 The woman and one girl are holding these in their hands.
9 The birthday girl is wearing this on her head.

10 These are on the people's feet.

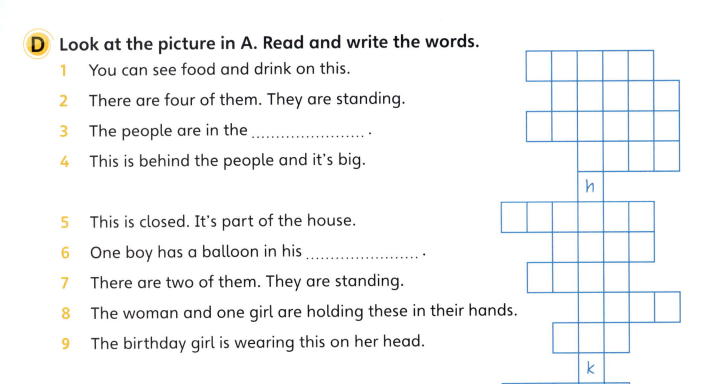

E Look at the pictures and write the words.

Example

s k i r t

1

_ _ _ _ _ _

2

_ _ _

_ _ _ _ _

3

_ _ _ _ _ _ _ _

4

_ _ _ _ _ _ _ _ _ _

What can you wear?

What can you eat?

What sport can you play?

F Read about Sam and Jill. Write the words from E.

33 `On the beach`

A Draw lines.

sand

sea

beach

ball

boat

sun

fish

bird

mat

water

shell

phone

monkey

B Answer questions about the picture.

C Find these things in the picture. Look at the letters. Write the words.

Example

c o c o n u t

1

t a h
c w

_ _ _ _ _

2

o f o
t

_ _ _ _ _

3

4

_ _ _ _ _ _ _

5

a n a
n
s b a

_ _ _ _ _ _

D What are the missing words?

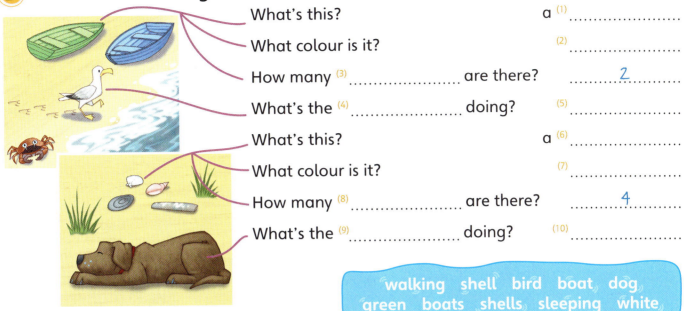

What's this?   a (1) ....

What colour is it?   (2) ....

How many (3) .... are there?   .... 2 ....

What's the (4) .... doing?   (5) ....

What's this?   a (6) ....

What colour is it?   (7) ....

How many (8) .... are there?   .... 4 ....

What's the (9) .... doing?   (10) ....

walking   shell   bird   boat   dog
green   boats   shells   sleeping   white

E ▶ Listen and draw lines.

      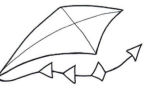

F Play the game! What's in your beach bag?

34 'Let's go to the park'

A Look at the picture and choose answers.

1	What is the big boy doing?	............*e*............	**a** kicking a ball
2	Who is running?	....	**b** the man
3	Who is waving?	....	**c** picking up a pear
4	What is the girl doing?	....	**d** the woman
5	What is the small boy doing?	....	**e** flying a kite

B Read the questions. Write one-word answers.

1 Who is kicking a ball?   the small ....
2 What is the man doing?   ....
3 Who is picking up a pear?   the ....
4 What is the woman doing?   ....
5 What is the big boy flying?   a ....

C 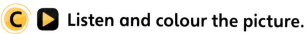 Listen and colour the picture.

D You're in the park! Read the questions and write answers.

1   How many people are in the park?   2   How many trees can you see? ......
3   Is it morning, afternoon or evening? ....
4   Who are you with? ....
5   What are you doing? ....
6   Which animals can you see? ....
7   What are you wearing? ....

E ▶ Read it! Write! Say it!

The park is great!
I can run, ...
and play!
With my ....!
Let's go to the park!

F Play the game! Animal sentences.

....

Team A	Team B

73

35 'What, who and where?'

A Complete the questions with **Who**, **What** or **Where**.
Write the answers to the questions.

1 ....'s this?   .... Tony ....
2 ....'s this?   a ....
3 ..... Where .....'s the camera?   in Tony's ....

1 Who's this?   ....
2 What's she got in her hand?   a ....
3 Where's the shell?   on her ....

B Question word spelling.

C Write **where** or **who** in the questions.

1 .... is angry?
2 .... are the girls?
3 .... are the clothes?
4 ....'s playing with a doll?

the mother
in Sue's bedroom
on the floor
the girls

D Write one-word answers.

②

5	Where are the clothes now?	under the ....
6	Where are the books now?	in the ....

③

7	Who's sitting on the bed?	the ....
8	Who's opening the cupboard?	the ....

E Questions about you.

What do you watch on TV? ....

Who watches TV with you? ....

Where is the television in your house? ....

What do you have for dinner? ....

Who has dinner with you? ....

Where do you have dinner? ....

What games do you play? ....

Who do you play with at school? ....

Where do you play in your school? ....

F ▶ Read, then listen and draw.

Monsters, monsters,

I love monsters!

My monster lamp, my monster mat, the monster on my bed.

The monsters in my toy box and the monsters on my wall.

Monsters, monsters, I love them all!

75

Great games, great hobbies!

A ▶ **What are the missing words? You choose! Then listen to the answers.**

Kim likes playing me in the ....evening............ . She sits on her (1) .... and plays me on her new (2) .... There's an old (3) .... in me. He's catching lots of small (4) .... They're swimming in the sea. Can you see the (5) .... on their tails? Can you see the (6) .... on the tree, too? It likes eating bananas!

Kim and her (7) .... are really good at playing me. They can listen to funny (8) .... on me, too. What am I? I'm a computer game!

B **Look at the letters and write the words.**

 Example
r o b o t

 o t o b r

 3 _ _ _ _

 e t k i

 1 _ _ _ _

 m g a e

 4 _ _ _ _ _

 n e l p a

 2 _ _ _ _

 t b a o

 5 _ _ _ _ _

 k y e o m n

 PROJECT

D **Which is Tom? Alex? Lucy? Read and draw lines.**

1

There's my friend, Tom! He enjoys fishing.

The boy with the red hair?

No! Tom's hair is black!

2

Alex is in this playground. She loves watching TV.

The girl in the blue dress?

No, Alex is wearing a yellow T-shirt.

3

Lucy is here, too. She likes swimming.

The girl with the kite?

No, Lucy's got a crocodile!

E **Play the game! We're making long words.**

37 Let's play

Look and read. Put a tick (✔) or a cross (✗) in the box.

Examples

This is a horse. ✔

This is a name. ✗

1 This is a television. ☐

2 This is a goat. ☐

3 This is a jacket. ☐

4 This is a bike. ☐

5 This is a football. ☐

B What can you do with a ball? Write **a**, **e**, **i**, **o** or **u**.

b__ __nc__ it!   c__tch it!   h__t it!   k__ck it!   thr__w it!

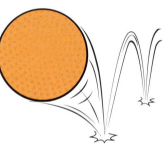

C Write letters, sports and names!

a	b	c	d	e

....

a	1	Alex is at the (beach) with his grandfather today. He loves ....*swimming*....!
☐	2	Anna goes to the (park.) She plays .... there.
☐	3	Sue enjoys watching .... on (television) with her family.
☐	4	Jill likes playing .... in the (playground) with her friends.
☐	5	Tony wants to play .... in the (garden) with his cousin Bill.

D ▶ Listen and tick (✔) the box.

Which is Ben's favourite sport?

A ✔   B ☐   C ☐

1 Which sport is Kim doing today?

A ☐   B ☐   C ☐

2 What is Lucy doing?

A ☐   B ☐   C ☐

3 What is Tom watching on TV?

A ☐   B ☐   C ☐

4 Where is Dan?

A ☐   B ☐   C ☐

5 Which girl is Sam?

A ☐   B ☐   C ☐

E *OK! Great!, Yes, please!* or *No, thanks!*

Let's play ....
Jill

Do you want to play ....
Tony

Would you like to play ....
Sue

F Play the game. Let's move!

38 My favourites

A **What are these?**

shoes, socks, trousers ....clothes..........

1   drawing, fishing, painting ....
2   blue, green, grey ....
3   cow, chicken, tiger ....
4   badminton, baseball, soccer ....
5   tomato, rice, grapes ....
6   robot, doll, teddy bear ....
7   milk, fruit juice, water ....

B **Ask and answer questions.**

	My favourite 🙂	.............'s favourite 🙂	.............'s favourite 🙂
animal	....	....	....
colour	....	....	....
drink	....	....	....
food	....	....	....
toy	....	....	....
sport	....	....	....
hobby	....	....	....

80

C **Look at the pictures. Complete the sentences about Lucy.**

Lucy is nine. Her favourite colour is ......*purple*...... and her favourite toy is her ....
She likes eating .... and drinking
....
Her favourite animal is a ....
She enjoys playing ....

D **Tell us about your friend. And your alien friend!**

.... is ....
His/Her favourite colour is .... and his/her favourite toy is his/her ....
He/She likes eating .... and drinking
....
His/Her favourite animal is a ....
He/She enjoys playing ....

E **Find and circle the American English words in the box. Then, write Pat's letter.**

s	o	c	c	e	r	f	l	f
p	t	r	e	g	r	a	y	r
c	o	l	o	r	k	v	t	i
a	s	f	c	s	t	o	r	e
n	e	r	a	s	e	r	u	s
d	v	x	m	z	b	i	c	u
y	a	i	w	q	y	t	k	f
a	p	a	r	t	m	e	n	t

Hello! My name's Tom!
I live in a **flat** next to a **sweet shop** in London. My Dad drives a big **grey lorry**. My **favourite** sport is **football**. I love the **colour** blue and I love eating **chips**!
Tell me about you!

Hi! I'm Pat.
I live in an .... next to a
.... in New York. My dad drives
a big ....
My favourite sport is .... I love
the .... blue and I love eating
.... !

F **Play the game! Let's make crosswords.**

39 'One foot, two feet'

(A) Look and read. Put a tick (✔) or a cross (✗) in the box.

Examples

 This is a house. ✔   This is a man. ✗

 1 This is a child. ☐   2 This is a balloon. ☐

 3 This is a foot. ☐   4 This is a mouse. ☐

 5 This is a person. ☐

(B) Complete the words.

<u>a m o u s e</u>   lots of mice
one foot   two f__ __t
a m__n   nine men
one woman   ten wom__n
a ch__ld   four children
one fish   lots of f__sh
a sh__ __p   seven sheep
one person   six p__ __ple

(C) Write yes or no.

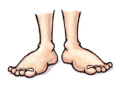 

There is one fish.   ......no......
1 There is one mouse.   ....
2 There is one woman.   ....
3 There is one foot.   ....
4 There are two men.   ....
5 There are two sheep.   ....
6 There are two children.   ....
7 There is one person.   ....

D Talk about the picture!

E Make sentences about the picture in D.

One	fish	are	eating	blue T-shirts.
Two	sheep	is	swimming	some bread.
Three	mice	are	running	a flower.
Four	people	are	eating	in the water.
Five	children	are	wearing	behind the dog.

F Look at the family and answer questions.

G Play the game! What's my word?

a	b	c	d	e	f	g	h	i	j	k	l	m
1	2	3	4	5	6	7	8	9	10	11	12	13
n	o	p	q	r	s	t	u	v	w	x	y	z
14	15	16	17	18	19	20	21	22	23	24	25	26

40 Night and day

A Write **morning**, **afternoon**, **evening** or **night**.

1  2  3  4

...........*morning*............ ....

B Find words.

b	n	b	h	a	v	e	l	u	n	c	h	b	g
g	g	o	t	o	s	c	h	o	o	l	b	n	o
e	h	a	v	e	l	e	s	s	o	n	s	d	t
t	d	h	a	v	e	a	b	a	t	h	b	b	o
u	h	a	v	e	d	i	n	n	e	r	d	n	b
p	b	b	g	o	t	o	s	l	e	e	p	b	e
h	a	v	e	b	r	e	a	k	f	a	s	t	d

C Write **in the** or **at**. Write words from B under parts of the day.

.... morning	.... afternoon	.... evening	.... night
	have lunch		

D ▶ Listen and write a name or a number.

What is the boy's name? ......*Tony*.....   How old is he? ....8.......

1 How many things are in Tony's school bag?   ....
2 What's the name of Tony's street?   .... Street.
3 What's the number of Tony's bus?   ....
4 Which class is Tony in?   ....
5 What's the name of Tony's teacher?   Mr ....

E Tony's morning. Listen and write numbers and words.

Tony's in his bedroom.

a 3

b 2

c 1

He goes to the bathroom.

d .... ☐

e .... ☐

f .... ☐

He finds his school clothes.

g .... ☐

h .... ☐

i .... ☐

He goes to the living room.

j .... ☐

k .... ☐

l .... ☐

He goes to the kitchen and has his breakfast.

m .... ☐

n .... ☐

o .... ☐

He goes to the hall and finds his school bag.

p .... ☐

q .... ☐

r .... ☐

Tony says 'Goodbye' to his ....

s

He opens the door, runs to the .... ,

t

sits next to his friend, Ben, and goes to ....

u

F Play the game! Change places.

41 Trains, boats and planes

A Make words with these letters.

rstuyabceiklnopq

b _ _   c _ _
b _ _ _   b _ _ _
p _ _ _ _   t _ _ _ _
t _ _ _ _   l _ _ _ _
m _ _ _ _ _ _ _ _ _
h _ _ _ _ _ _ _ _ _ _

B Look at the pictures, read the questions and write answers.

Examples:

How many children are there? ....2.............

What are the children riding?   their ......bikes......

1   How many birds can you see?   ....

2   Where are the children now? at the ....
3   What is the woman driving?   a ....

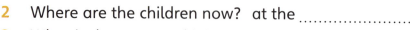
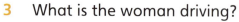

4   What is the boy painting?   a ....
5   What is the girl doing?   ....

C ▶ **Listen and tick (✔) the box.**

Example: What is Pat wearing today?

A ☐   B ☐   C ✔

1 Which boy is Bill?

A ☐   B ☐   C ☐

2 Which sport is Sam playing?

A ☐   B ☐   C ☐

3 What is Tom doing?

A ☐   B ☐   C ☐

4 Where is Mum?

A ☐   B ☐   C ☐

5 How does Alex come to school?

A ☐   B ☐   C ☐

D **Talk about the picture. What can you see?**

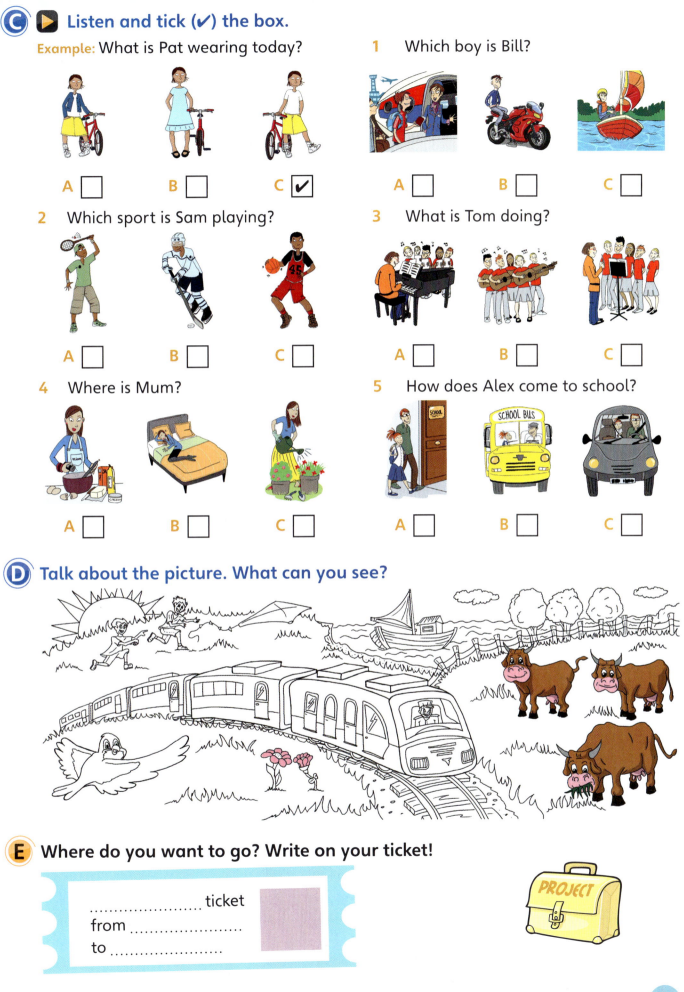

E **Where do you want to go? Write on your ticket!**

.... ticket

from ....

to ....

PROJECT

87

42 About a phone

A **What can you see? Write the words.**

..........friends.......... ....

....

B **Read this. Choose and write the correct word from A next to numbers 1–5.**

People talk to their ......friends...... with me. You can find
me in a store in a (1) .... in front of Mrs Bean's
house. Some people put me on a (2) .... ,
but Mrs Bean puts me in her brown (3) ....
Mrs Bean is a teacher at Lucy's (4) .... I'm very
small. I have letters and (5) .... on me.

What am I? I am a phone.

C **Say it!**

I'm taking photos of me and my friend with my phone!

D Put the bus on the street!

Phones For Me

E ▶ Listen and colour the phones.

F Look at the picture and write the words.

1 There are six .... _windows_ .... in the houses.
2 I can see three .... in this picture.
3 There are five .... in the street.
4 I can see four .... in Mrs Bean's garden.
5 There are two .... in the fruit shop window.
6 I can see seven .... in this picture.
7 There is one .... in the car.

G Play the game! Listen, spell and answer.

43 What are they saying?

A Which picture? Read the sentences. Write the number of the picture.

1

Goodbye.

2

These are yours.

Thank you.

3

Bye!

4

This is yours.

Thanks.

1	This is a boat.	Picture ....3.......
2	This is a dog.	Picture ....
3	This is a robot.	Picture ....
4	This is a teacher.	Picture ....

B In which picture are they saying ...

goodbye?   Picture .... and ....
thank you?   Picture .... and ....

C Write **his**, **hers** or **theirs**.

This dog is mine.

1   The flowers are ....
2   The dog is ....
3   The boat is ....

D Draw lines between the two sentences about a person in the picture in E.

1   This young man is holding a present.
2   This woman is giving a burger to a small boy.
3   This man is waving goodbye to his grandmother.
4   This man has got a red bag. It's open and some clothes and two bottles are on the ground.
5   This old man is listening to a young boy.

a   He's standing next to the train.
b   He's wearing a grey jacket and brown shoes.
c   He's standing in front of the burger store.
d   She's got long brown hair and she's wearing pink trousers.
e   He's wearing glasses.

E Look at the picture. Draw lines.

Happy birthday.

Thank you.

Bye!

Pardon?

See you!

Oh dear!

Thanks.

Here you are.

F ▶ Listen and make the conversations.

G Play the game! What's on my card?

44 'About us'

A Make questions for the girl to answer.

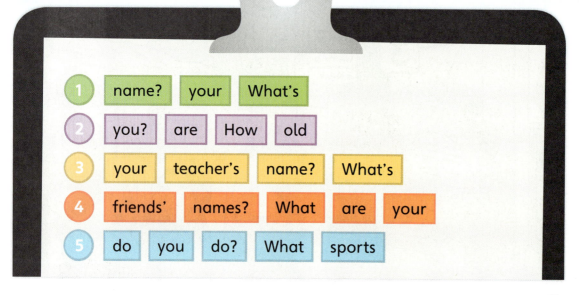

1. name? your What's
2. you? are How old
3. your teacher's name? What's
4. friends' names? What are your
5. do you do? What sports

▶ Listen and write the girl's answers.

1 ....   2 ....

3 Miss ....   4 Anna and ....

5 swimming and ....

B Which is the right answer? Draw lines.

Show me your beautiful picture.   Dad's cleaning them.

Give me your dirty shoes!   Or some chocolate ones?

Sing me a sad song, please!   Right! Here! Catch it!

Ask me a question.   How do you spell your name?

Throw me that red ball, please!   Which book is it in?

Make me some lemon cakes!   I only know happy ones!

Read me that funny story again!   He loves drawing aliens.

Tell me about your brother.   It's a yellow flower. Look!

C Listen and tick (✔) the box.

1 Kim lives in a ... .

A ☐ B ☐

2 She goes to ... School.

A ☐ B ☐ C ☐

3 Kim is in class number ... .

11 **7** **12**

A ☐ B ☐ C ☐

4 Kim's eyes are ... .

A ☐ B ☐ C ☐

5 Her hair is ... .

A ☐ B ☐ C ☐

6 Kim plays the ... .

A ☐ B ☐

7 Kim's books are in the ... .

A ☐ B ☐ C ☐

8 Kim's favourite stories are about ... .

A ☐ B ☐ C ☐

D Write and talk about Nick.

E Write about you.

F Play bingo! About us!

45 'Happy ending!'

A Look at the pictures. Write the words.

```
                              p       q
                              [ ]     u[ ][ ][ ]
                    a         [ ]
                    [ ]       c r o s s w o r d
                    [ ]
              w     [ ]       n[ ][ ]
        g[ ][ ][ ]  s
              [ ]    k[ ][ ]  c           m
              [ ]    [ ]      [ ]         [ ]
        l            [ ]    o[ ][ ]       [ ]
      t[ ][ ]        i[ ]              z
                                         [ ]
    a l p h a b e t       j[ ]          y[ ]
              [█]         e[ ][ ][ ]
    r[ ]      f[ ]
                          [ ]
              d[ ][ ]
                          [ ]
```

B Make word groups.

| wall | ~~clean~~ | they | kite | sea | two | | ~~green~~ | night | tree | you | hall | say |

bean	day	right	three	zoo	ball
clean	....	....	....	....	....
green	....	....	....	....	....

1

2

3

C Play the circles game!

the end

z you see animals here

y not old

w you do this with your feet

v you are .... good

u not beautiful

t you play this

s you do this in water

q go to **n**

p you eat this

r you listen to this

o a colour and a fruit

k you do this in football

n not day

j you wear this

m an animal

i you eat this

go to **n**

l you eat this

h part of your body

go to **c**

g your mother's father

f lives in water

e you eat this

b you play this

c an animal

d children play with these

a part of a day

the start

95

11   Whose is it?

Learner A
Write the words for the pictures. Put a tick (✔) beside the things you have
and a cross (✗) beside the things you don't have.

picture	words	Me	....
	....		
	....		
	....		
	....		
	....		
	....		
	....		
	....		
	....		
	....		

15 One, two, three animals.

Write all the animals on the zoo sign.

24 What's the class doing?

Learner A

11   Whose is it?

Learner B

Write the words for the pictures. Put a tick (✔) beside the things you have and a cross (✘) beside the things you don't have.

picture	words	Me	....
	....		
	....		
	....		
	....		
	....		
	....		
	....		
	....		
	....		
	....		

24   What's the class doing?

Learner B

25   Animal challenge

What can you see in the animal picture on page 54?
Put a tick (✔) or a cross (✗) in the box.

Can you see the crocodile's tail?	✔	the giraffe's face?	✗
1 the spider's body?		6 the giraffe's feet?	
2 the tiger's nose?		7 the fish's tail?	
3 the hippo's legs?		8 the bird's eyes?	
4 the monkey's arms?		9 the crocodile's mouth?	
5 the elephant's head?		10 the giraffe's ears?	

35   What, who and where?

41   Trains, boats and planes

What's this?

What's this?

Unit wordlist

1

animals

cat ....

dog ....

duck ....

fish ....

frog ....

goat ....

sheep ....

snake ....

spider ....

school

alphabet ....

letter ....

verbs

draw ....

say ....

spell ....

questions

What's this? ....

2

numbers

one ....

two ....

three ....

four ....

five ....

six ....

seven ....

eight ....

nine ....

ten ....

eleven ....

twelve ....

thirteen ....

fourteen ....

fifteen ....

sixteen ....

seventeen ....

eighteen ....

nineteen ....

twenty ....

possessions

ball ....

book ....

football ....

toy ....

clothes

shoe ....

sock ....

verbs

colour ....

write ....

3

names

family name ....

Miss ....

Mr ....

Mrs ....

name ....

the home

address ....

street ....

time

birthday ....

possessive adjectives

her ....

his ....

its ....

questions

How do you
spell that? ....

4

colours

black ....

blue ....

brown ....

green ....

gray/grey ....

orange ....

pink ....

purple ....

red ....

white ....

yellow ....

animals

bird ....

the home

tree ....

possessions

bike ....

boat ....

kite ....

verbs

paint ....

questions

What colour
is your hair? ....

What colour
are your eyes? ....

5

school

box ....

cross ....

example ....

line ....

no ....

question ....

sentence ....

test ....

tick ....

word ....

yes ....

possessions

paints ....

watch ....

animals

lizard ....

verbs

answer ....

put ....

tick ....

6

body and face

arm ....

body ....

ear ....

eye ....

face ....

foot ....

hair ....

hand ....

head ....

leg ....

mouth ....

nose ....

tail ....

animals

crocodile ....

elephant ....

giraffe ....

horse ....

mouse ....

zoo ....

adjectives

big ....

long ....

small ....

7

possessions

computer ....

keyboard ....

robot ....

animals

monkey ....

verbs

listen ....

look ....

run ....

see ....

sit ....

smile ....

throw the dice ....

wave ....

8

clothes

bag ....

dress ....

handbag ....

hat ....

jacket ....

jeans ....

shirt ....

skirt ....

trousers ....

T-shirt ....

home

chair ....

lamp ....

verbs

wear ....

adjectives

favourite ....

new ....

9

the home

flower ....

wall ....

school

story ....

verbs

drink ....

have got ....

hold ....

learn about ....

like ....

love ....

read ....

adjectives

beautiful ....

funny ....

happy ....

sad ....

ugly ....

adverbs

really ....

very ....

10

family

brother ....

cousin ....

dad ....

father ....

grandfather ....

grandma ....

grandmother ....

grandpa ....

grandparent ....

mother ....

mum ....

parent ....

sister ....

the home

flat ....

garden ....

house ....

other nouns

circle ....

verbs

live ....

prepositions

with ....

possessive adjectives

our ....

their ....

pronouns

this ....

these ....

11

possessions

balloon ....

beach ball ....

camera ....

clock ....

(computer) mouse ....

doll ....

drawing ....

guitar ....

phone ....

picture ....

radio ....

tennis ball ....

sports and leisure

drawing ....

music ....

verbs

fish ....

possessive pronouns

hers ....

his ....

questions

Whose is this? ....

expressions

Pardon? ....

Sorry? ....

12

people

baby ....

best friend ....

boy ....

children ....

girl ....

man ....

men ....

people ....

person ....

woman ....

women ....

conjunctions

or ....

expressions

Good afternoon! ....

Good morning! ....

Hello! ....

Good! ....

Great! ....

Oh! ....

OK! ....

Wow! ....

13

people

monster ....

verbs

can ....

catch fish ....

draw pictures ....

fly ....

have a swimming lesson ....

jump ....

play badminton ....

play tennis ....

play the guitar ....

ride a bike ....

ride a horse ....

run ....

sing ....

spell really long words ....

swim ....

take photos ....

write songs ....

adjectives

good at ....

conjunctions

and ....

but ....

14

adjectives

clean ....

dirty ....

happy ....

long ....

new ....

old ....

sad ....

short ....

young ....

verbs

smile ....

questions

What's this? ....

What are these? ....

15

animals

chicken ....

cow ....

hippo ....

tiger ....

sports and leisure

ball game ....

game ....

verbs

walk ....

prepositions

in ....

next to ....

on ....

under ....

16

food and drink

apple ....

banana ....

bean ....

carrot ....

coconut ....

egg ....

fruit ....

grape ....

lemon ....

lemonade ....

lime ....

mango ....

milk ....

onion ....

orange ....

pea ....

pear ....

pineapple ....

pizza ....

potato ....

tomato ....

vegetable ....

watermelon ....

verbs

eat ....

adjectives

round ....

17

food and drink

bread ....

burger ....

café ....

chicken ....

chips ....

chocolate cake ....

egg ....

fish ....

fries ....

hot chocolate ....

ice cream ....

juice ....

rice ....

sausage ....

water ....

verbs

add ....

make a drink ....

try ....

adverbs

today ....

questions

What would
you like? ....

18

the home
bathroom ....
bedroom ....
bookcase ....
desk ....
dining room ....
hall ....
home ....
kitchen ....
living room ....
mat ....
mirror ....
room ....
table leg ....
television ....

prepositions
like ....

questions
Where's your home? ....

19

the home
armchair ....
bed ....
board ....
cup ....
cupboard ....
floor ....
phone ....
piano ....
wall ....
window ....

verbs
complete ....

20

the home
sofa ....

places
bookshop ....
park ....
shop ....

adjectives
closed ....
open ....
tall ....

prepositions
behind ....
in front of ....

determiners
lots of ....
many ....
no ....

21

transport
bike ....
boat ....
bus ....
car ....
helicopter ....
lorry ....
motorbike ....
plane ....
train ....
truck ....

verbs
move ....
start ....
stop ....

adverbs
again ....
here ....
there ....

22

school
classroom ....
eraser ....
page ....
pen ....
pencil ....
playground ....
rubber ....
ruler ....
schoolbag ....
teacher ....

verbs
draw lines ....
take to school ....
wear glasses ....

pronouns
that ....
those ....

school
blackboard ....
class ....
English book ....
glasses case ....
painting ....
pencil case ....
student ....
whiteboard ....

verbs
learn English ....
sit next to ....

possessive adjectives
her ....
his ....
my ....
our ....
their ....
your ....

questions
Whose is this? ....

transport
rocket ....

verbs
do a crossword ....
fish ....
go to bed ....
have a bath ....
listen to the teacher ....
make a plane ....
phone ....
point ....

sit down ....
throw a ball ....
write music ....

adjectives
double ....

food and drink
meat ....

animal
fly ....
insect ....

the world around us
grass ....
plant ....

adjectives
fat ....
wild ....

verbs
get milk ....

animals
pet mice ....

places
television studios ....

verbs
ask ....
talk ....

questions
How many ....
How old ....
Which pets would
you like to have? ....

food and drink
breakfast ....
dinner ....
lunch ....
supper ....
sweets ....

verbs
have for breakfast ....
I don't know. ....
want ....

28
food and drink
menu ....

time
day ....

verbs
drink for lunch ....
eat for breakfast ....
say ....

29
places
toy shop ....

verbs
clean ....
do ....
hold ....
sit ....
sleep ....
stand ....

adjectives
tired ....

adverbs
now ....

prepositions
between ....

30
the home
bathroom door ....
hall table ....

verbs
choose ....
pick up ....
watch TV ....

prepositions
on the wall ....
with four legs ....

31
transport
school bus ....

verbs
close ....
come to school ....
drive a car ....
fly a plane ....
go home ....
open ....
ride a motorbike ....

adjectives
nice ....

prepositions
by (bike/car) ....

questions
How do you ....
come to school? ....

32
birthdays
birthday cake ....
party ....
present ....

time
year ....

verbs
give ....

expressions
Happy birthday! ....

33
the world around us
beach ....
cloud ....
sand ....
sea ....
shell ....

clothes
beach bag ....

weather
sun ....

questions

What do you take
to the beach? ....

What do you wear
to the beach? ....

animals

zebra ....

verbs

choose answers ....

open a sweet ....

phone a friend ....

sing a song ....

questions

How many people
are in the park? ....

What is the boy doing? ....

Who is waving? ....

expressions

Let's go to the park! ....

adjectives

angry ....

right ....

verbs

have dinner ....

play with dolls ....

prepositions

on TV ....

pronouns

that ....

this ....

questions

What? ....

Where? ....

Who? ....

sports and leisure

computer game ....

hobby ....

screen ....

body and face

teeth ....

verbs

enjoy ....

swim in the sea ....

sports

badminton ....

baseball ....

basketball ....

hockey ....

table tennis ....

tennis ....

verbs

bounce ....

catch ....

go fishing ....

go swimming ....

hit ....

kick ....

prepositions

at the beach ....

on television ....

expressions

Great! ....

No, thanks! ....

Yes, please! ....

sports and leisure

drawing ....

fishing ....

hockey stick ....

painting ....

toys

teddy bear ....

British and American words

chips – fries ....

colour – color ....

favourite – favorite ....

flat – apartment ....

football – soccer ....

grey – gray ....

lorry – truck ....

shop – store ....

sweet – candy ....

toys

alien ....

39

irregular plurals

child – children ....

fish – fish ....

foot – feet ....

man – men ....

mouse – mice ....

person – people ....

sheep – sheep ....

woman – women ....

40

time

afternoon ....

day ....

evening ....

morning ....

night ....

verbs

get up ....

go to sleep ....

put on clothes ....

say goodbye ....

wash ....

prepositions

at night ....

in the morning ....

questions

When? ....

41

transport

ticket ....

wheel ....

verbs

play hockey ....

prepositions

at the beach ....

in our car ....

on the bus ....

from ....

to ....

42

places

phone shop ....

shop door ....

store ....

verbs

find ....

take photos of a friend ....

talk to a friend ....

adjectives

correct ....

prepositions

at school ....

in a store ....

expressions

Right! ....

43

food and drink

bottle ....

burger store ....

places

station ....

verbs

wave goodbye ....

expressions

Bye! ....

Don't worry! ....

Goodbye ....

Good evening ....

Here you are. ....

I don't understand. ....

Me too! ....

Oh dear! ....

See you! ....

That's right. ....

Well done! ....

personal pronouns

I	me	
he	him	
she	her	
it	it	its ....
we	us	ours ....
you	you	
they	them	

44

verbs

ask a question ....

make a cake ....

read a lot ....

show me a picture ....

tell us a story ....

try new food ....

write stories ....

write with your
left hand ....

prepositions

about ....

45

sports and leisure

counter ....

dice ....

end ....

start ....

body and face

part of your body ....

school

letters of the ....
alphabet ....

time

part of the day ....

verbs

clap ....

questions

What now? ....